ABOUT THE AUTHOR

Born into a loving Irish Catholic family, where communicating with the spirit world was not only a sin but blasphemy, to speak of what Jane saw as a child was considered dark and evil. Jane spent most of her childhood dreading bedtime for that was when she would relax and experience other worldly dimensions. Unable to articulate what she would experience, she suppressed her gifts to the best of her abilities. Throughout Jane's successful military career and motherhood, it became apparent she could no longer suppress her gifts and had to learn, during her own spiritual journey, not only to control but to embrace and love her abilities. Jane now is able to see the beauty, healing and honour of her work and is humbled to be able to share her writings.

I have two very special people to thank, my wonderful friend Andrea for her help, support and laughter. Without your help and editing skills, I certainly wouldn't be attempting to release another book. The ability to open your mind to how I write, which has been a challenge for such a scientific questioning person. Thank you my lovely!

Gorgeous Gareth always appears when I need him, an amazing, talented and spiritually gifted person. You gave me the strength and confidence to push forward when I doubted myself. You shared your knowledge and gave me the tools to continue my journey. Thank you so much!

MYSTIC MOMENTS IN LOVE AND LIGHT

When two worlds become one

Jane Lee
Vol. 2

ISBN-13: 9798565339697

Cover design by: Gareth van Rensburg
Library of Congress Control Number: 2018675309
Printed in the United States of America

CONTENTS

A Balloon

A balloon floating high in the sky
It floats so high, it's out of sight
Where does that balloon go?
The balloon continues further than the eye
For many unexplainable occurrences cannot be seen
Left to the imagination to explore.
The wonders of the imagination
A world where anything truly exists.
It's up to the person's imagination to explore
Only limited by oneself and the lack of self permission
To take things a little further.
Our minds are so beautiful
Yet such little of it used
Scientifically proven, we only use a small percentage
How about exploring our minds
Freeing the boundaries and floating free
Like the balloon?
Who knows where that balloon has gone?

A Bucket

An object that collects soil or water
Moving substances from one area to another
If not emptied, can become over full
Spill over at the edges
Even crack if the weight becomes too heavy
Whilst carrying the load upon one's back.
The mighty bucket in some communities is life saving
In other countries unvalued
Left to crack and rot outside.
The bucket
Which type of bucket would you choose for another?
One for survival or one to crumble with the demands
of life, overflowing?
It is just as important to empty the bucket as to fill
Maybe a world where one could help
Unload the burden of another by listening.
In another country donate unwanted possessions
Which would help give and fill the buckets for survival.

A Candle

Look at the wick burning brightly
Powerful on the eye, strong and mighty.
Not to be touched
Could get burnt
Intriguing the candle light
Mesmerising and captivating.
For many a meditation has been focused on the
simplicity
Of the light of a candle
Everyone needs a little escapism
Everyone needs a little light
Even if just from a candle here.

A Channel

A channel of peace
To filter out negativity, anger and hatred
To allow only pure light and love to filter through
What a discipline
For many this is unattainable
But for you a must
You are a channel of peace
You are special and honourable
Accept the responsibility with pride in your heart
You will always be honest and see the truth in all
For your eyes are wise and see honesty in all
The good, the bad, the grey areas too
You have the ability to filter through.
Filter what is acceptable, disregard the unpleasant-
ness
Not to judge the error of others' ways
But to stop them filtering through to you.
Continue to filter the light energy to all
For you have been chosen to channel through.

A Cuppa

It's not just a cuppa one craves
It's the company present
A cuppa and a chat is so precious
Invokes conversations unexpected
But most of all in the right company, companionship
A friend even
The most precious gift you can give another Time!
Time is so precious in this busy world often of
self-importance
How good does it feel to spend time with another light
hearted soul?
It feels good
All through the suggestion of making time for a cuppa.
Society is changing so quickly
Once a common occurrence to boil the kettle
Now a world where one has to schedule the time in
Society will continue to change but basic human in-
stincts
don't
Human contact is vital for the welfare of us all
So go on, put the kettle on.

A Cushion

Will you be my cushion?
When all around is crumbling
And I feel I'm going to collapse to the ground.
Will you be my cushion?
A warm cosy, fluffed up cushion
To break my fall
Absorb my tears and shelter my face.
A cushion to hide behind
When I am scared
A cushion to hide the tear streaked marks.
Will you be my cushion, who cares?

A Fence

So many build a fence around oneself
It will keep the outside world away
I can protect my young, keep them safe
Shut the world away
From my innocent children.
No need to see the unpleasantness on the streets
Certainly not going to let them
Mix with the poor, the uneducated
No certainly not.
This sounds so hypocritical
But how many of us secretly think like this?
How will the young spread their innocence and light
Among the wounded?
To teach there is kindness, protection and safety
Yes it does exist
If we don't share?
Our young must be given the opportunity to witness all
aspects of life
To empathize
For without understanding of the world
Our young are imprisoned within this life
A life of very little
A life which consists of little learning and appreciation
That's not living

Allow the children freedom to witness all of life.
It's called the education of life for a reason.

A Flicker Of Hope

A flicker of hope, is all one needs
To gain momentum upon one's feet
To hope to walk the path of light
Be amazed by all the wondrous delights.
This world is precious to all that hope
Hope of a land
Where all will be glad
Glad to share love to another
Diminish the burdens and worries of one another
Filter our air with words of light
And energy so uplifting to all that surround
Hope!
Hope that one day this world will exist
Where man can live in harmony
A harmony so balanced that all can share our clean air.
For this new world will consist
Of trees in abundance
Nature and animals roaming free
Organic and beauty for every eye
That will notice the passing of time.
Value, the value to stop and stare
And make peace with every soul who wishes to care.
For peace on earth
Will one day be true.
Not just a virtual reality manufactured.

As two worlds emerge into one
The lessons of love
Will have begun.
For no one can turn their cheek away from the truth
That one day
My love these words
Will be reality.

A Humming Bird

Tiny, the humming bird
Something mesmerising about this fragile creature
Beautiful and pleasing to the eye
Appears gentle, nurturing and kind.
All of these comments summarised from what we see
Now let's look at the reality
The humming bird is quick and strong
Continues to hum along
Will lure you in with false pretence
Then swipe your twigs
From your nest
Better to judge from afar
For some humans also appear to be a farse
Different from what one might perceive
Always invest time in others
For not to, would be wrong
But look closely at how they behave
The words from the mouths throughout the days
Look by all means but don't forget to sense the true
person.
The true person will be hidden inside
Better to ruffle the feathers than waste one's time.

A Necklace

An item of jewellery to enhance an outfit
Make you feel more presentable to the world
How do you feel at the end of the day when you remove
your
glitzy necklace?
For some plain, others a relief
For so many like to conform to society
Unfortunately one judges another on the way they look.
Not all, but many.
So many different souls and personalities
So many need the reassurance of the finery
Some souls really don't care.
Breathtakingly refreshing to have such a diversity of humans
Makes the world so interesting and alive
Never condemn the conformist or the free spirit
Embrace all, for all are unique and make this world
One of beauty and reflection.

A Snail

Look how gracious the slimy snail is
Not attractive to so many
Look a little closer
Difficult for the lack of nature lover.
It has everything
A sturdy home and where you get one
Always surrounded by many.
Slowly the snail goes
Determined little fellow
Never falters of his path
Gets there in the end.
Even when the mighty, ferocious birds come pecking
He'll hold his ground
For what he believes is honest and true
He believes in life
One day at a time and not rushing
But enjoying the journey.
Quite a clever creature
Don't you think?

A Thought

A thought will come your way
Don't block it or question it
Absorb it first
Then think
How will this thought benefit many?
Whether that is financially or lifting the energy.
What will you gain from it?
You're important too.
If you are happy
All those who surround you will feed off your vitality
Thoughts are to be absorbed processed and then the
decision
is yours.
Act upon or disregard?
The choice is yours
It is how you process these thoughts that
Either hinder or progress you upon your path.
All I will say is, if a thought is mighty and feels good
And could perhaps benefit others and most important
yourself
Go for it!

A Tiger

A graceful animal
With passion and very alive
Camouflaged amongst his habitat
So unaware by so many.
So much strength and talent
But so many unaware
Silently waiting for the right moment
The time will come
When the mighty tiger will surface.

So many unaware of what the tiger is capable of
Until the time is right
The silent unassuming tiger
Who kept quiet
Amongst the tall reeds
Was over looked and often over shadowed
By the loud laughing hyena's
For the hyenas
Would highlight their potential and shout from the
roofs
How talented they are and all they would achieve.
Surprise, surprise the talking hyena
Never evolved past the first hurdle
But the silent tiger
Who worked his way through

Pounced on his opportunity and was successful.

The moral of the story

Work hard, strive, never gloat and you will be rewarded.

A Time To Share

Buried deep within
A memory of regret, a guilt and shame
All buried secretly within
Never to be spoken of again.
I will take this secret and shame to my dying days.
A whole life consisting of a hidden shame
A burden carried upon your shoulders
Never able to enjoy this life fully
As there's a secret guilt
Hidden so well within
Your choice!
Carry that sordid secret of shame or take the risk
To eliminate that rainy day?
The cold and damp created within
Could be made to feel warm and content instead.
What should you do?
Nothing in life, cannot be overcome
A sharing and telling to another will help you over-
come.
The relief of saying those few harrowing words
Will lift you
To heavens and escapism you have never known
A world where your shoulders are finally free
To walk this path in harmony
Lightly on one's feet

Time to choose?

A Wounded Soul

A wounded soul walks by
Nobody notices the turmoil inside
But yet they continue to walk by
Acknowledge the lonely, say hello
For who knows with time the wounded soul
May release the hurt inside
Release it out into the open with time.
A wounded soul can only heal if they let go of the anguish
hidden deep
Next time you see a person all alone
Whose energy feels low
Smile, acknowledge and be kind
Who knows they might free themselves in time.
To simply acknowledge a fellow human in despair
Shows our human instinct
To share.

Aggression

Shouting, swearing, hand gestures and threatening behaviour
All a lack of control.
Something so simple finally takes you over the edge
A usually kind, patient, giving person behaves with inner
ugliness.
Will later reflect, analyse and feel, if humble
Regret.
Some will choose to ignore
Justify their behaviour to another
But you can't quite justify it to yourself
Not if you are to be totally honest?
If an apology would be a sign of weakness or admitting
you were wrong
Well at least acknowledge to yourself you weren't kind
Self accept and move on.

Aliens

We are all so fascinated by the possibility and exist-
ence of
aliens
It's not rocket science for there are billions of
undiscovered planets out there.
Of course there is another life form
For one would be deluded not to at least be open to it.
Scientists already know the answers
Have the evidence and all the technology
Just the timing is not quite right for exposure
But will come with time.
Not for us to worry at present
As we are fast becoming aliens to one another
Not giving one another human contact and time.
Let's concentrate
On the human aliens who are isolated through
Poverty, mental dis-ease and low self worth
Let's look after our wounded
Aliens who have become, alienated from society.

All The Lonely People

All the lonely people
Where do they all come from?
Historically there have always been lonely people
It's nothing new.
But this century is new
For what was a natural occurrence statistically has
spiralled out of control.
An unheard generation, left to rot
Unnoticed by many
Only noticed when one becomes intolerant
Or dementia sets in offending a passer-by
Who can be bothered to report?
Oh yes we are very good at reporting another
Not always caring for another.
Too many consumed in the land of fantasy
Making virtual friends
What have we allowed ourselves to become?
Maybe all of the above from loneliness
Better to have a virtual friend than a real one?
I'm not sure, are you?

Always Care

Be passionate about the young one's care
For their voice isn't often heard
The louder children with often less insecurities
Will always be heard.

The quiet child
Who's sensitive and aware
Who notices the negative comment and vibrations in the
air
Will sit quietly and stare.
Cry occasionally
As the vibrations of others emotions become too much
But once again the quiet, well behaved child
Will sit quietly and stare.

So when as a parent you worry about your young
Remember to give lots of reassurance
Make time to stop and stare.
You as the parent have your Child's best interest at heart
So never doubt the motion
You will take on their path.
Help the children grow up and be wise.

To respect we are all different and one of a kind.

Amethyst

A beautiful purple stone, some call a crystal
A crystal in its raw state consists of many facets.
Each facet ricochets energy in all directions
Some believe the Amethyst is a spiritual stone
Of protection, creativity and love.
Humans are like crystals
In their natural state
Reflecting emotions, thoughts, and actions onto one
another.
Funny how when you strip things back to basics,
How we were intended
Everything is quite simplistic.
We may have evolved in the fineries and material-
istic
But all living species are basic
We all consist of energy
It's how we choose to use our energies,
Give to others freely in light
To spread from one to another
Or hold in and consume?
Eventually if one consumes too long
One will combust, surely?
Another universal law
Whatever one releases

One will receive in return.
If one consumes and doesn't give off
The body, mind and spirit cannot function in harmony,
Karma.

Angels

I feel your presence
Day and night
Such a comfort to have you by my side
When worries arise
I send a thought
And although I worry
It's always sort.
I thank you for your presence in times of need
For you are my angel
Who stands by me
Never interfering unless sent for
All through a thought.
Thoughts of good intention
Are more powerful than one could comprehend
So remember these words
For some might mock
All is so real
Although may be not physical.
For the angels are sent from above
To walk the paths we have been chosen for.
Never question or question if you choose
Perhaps send a thought?

Another Year

Another year goes by
Where did that go?
A celebration of a birthday
A Child's birthday
Makes you reflect.
I can't believe so and so's
How old, I remember him as a baby.
Celebrate every year
Every year of life, so precious
As you all are
So much to learn and discover
Such little time.
Don't let the years run away
Capture and make use of them
Not to become so absorbed in your life
You miss the passing of time.
By this I mean
The seasons, the aging parents and the child's
milestones
Celebrate every year.

As Free As A Bird

Soaring through the sky
Gliding in the wind
Hopping from roof tops
Freedom.
Or so it appears
Still have to find food
Still have to feather the nest
Prepare for the storm and the harsh realities of winter.
So is this true freedom?
Yes for there is always choice.
For many there is none
For the elements of nature or manmade wars and cruelty
Have taken all.
I'd rather be the bird, fending off the realities of life
Than have the option taken from me.
Think!
How lucky we all our to have such insignificant worries
Be thankful.

Ask

Dare to ask
Whether it be a question or for help
Ask
Don't hinder your development by being afraid to ask.
No question is insignificant
For there are so many answers and elaborations to each.
You asking will evoke a greater understanding to the reciprocate
The reciprocate will understand more about you
How you think, what makes you who you are.
Communication is vital
As the presence of two spending time together
Can be invigorating, healing and also reflecting.
Choose who you spend time with
What energies best suit you
But beware of those, one must ration oneself to.
Never turn your back on a hindered soul
If your energy starts to feel depleted
Then ration.
As everything in life is good for us
Just needs a little rationing.

Autumn

Autumn what a beautiful time of year
The rich golden browns, yellows and reds
Something so striking about the array of autumn colours
So rich and warm.
The weather starting to change
A nip of cold in the air
The damp moist soil beneath one's feet
Makes one feel like hibernating from the elements
A feeling of wrapping up warm and escaping to the comfort of home
Families spending more time together under the same roof
Often bickering and squabbling.
Right get your coats on, out you go
For all must venture out into the open air
Wrap up warm, get those boots on
It's time to stop and stare
The air is fresh
The wind will bring you alive and you might even notice
the birds flying by.
This fresh air will bring a relief from within
As all need freedom to roam this beautiful place
Once back in doors

The irritation of each other has gone
Now where were we?
Oh yes, let us snuggle up once again indoors.

Be Kind To Yourself

Be kind to yourself
Who's the person who ridicules you the most?
Who's the hardest on one's self?
Who will always find fault when there is none present?
Who can always do better because it's not quite perfect?
Sound like anyone you might know?
Sounds in fact like many
Perhaps YOU!
Go easy on yourself just for today
Notice all the good things about you
If you only find few then I ask you to look at another you
admire
As you look you will see a reflection of yourself
For all the things you like in another
Are also in you
You just have never allowed yourself the time to reflect.
If you look with open eyes you will be surprised
How amazing you truly are and what others also see with
clarity in you.
So just for today go easy on yourself
Be kind, forgiving and see the beauty within

For you are a gift from above
Special and unique.
Remember there is only one of you.

Beauty

Beauty is in the beholder
Beauty within, beauty without and beauty in everything
It's how you perceive the world.
A beautiful landscape surrounded by roaming hills
A glistening lake and the hundred year old oaks
Beautifully organic.
Now the destruction of a storm, flood damaged roads
and destruction
Maybe not so beautiful?
But look what it could resemble
A clearing of the old stagnate energy
And the rebirth of a vibrant community with time.
A community that once didn't know one another
Now all know each other
Even better, connect on an emotional level.
It's how we perceive each obstacle throughout life
But one thing is for sure
What appears a negative
I'm yet to find one that some light hasn't filtered through
Whether that be, a stronger bond between man, a

teaching or Simply humbleness.

Bicycle

Look how the bicycle wheels go round and round
Powered by yourself
Will only stop if you put on the brakes
But as one knows you must apply gentle pressure on
the brakes
If not, you will tumble over the handle bars and come
to a grinding stop
Perhaps hurt yourself, maybe your pride.
It's healthy to get back on one's bike
For we all need the wind in our hair, the rain upon our
faces
The gentle touch and warmth of the sun.
We need to experience the bumps upon the path
The occasional pot hole
To truly enjoy the smooth times
Remember one thing
You have complete control on the turning of the
wheels
As well as the pressure you apply to the brakes
All within your control.

Birthday

Another year
Where does time go?
But time does go and yes so quickly
So precious time
As are you.
So it's your birthday
Maybe spent on your own
Or maybe with many.
Enjoy and embrace your special day
For you have put all your loving energy
Not only on our planet
But touched the hearts and souls of many
By simply, being you.
Thank you.

Blue

Blue held within the sky
Blue worn within the soul
Blue, such a healing colour
One that can't be made by mixing two colours.
Blue, some say, resembles the cold
How much beauty is held in the cold?
The delicate icicles upon the trees
The crisp, wet, damp grass upon one's feet.
Blue can resemble anything you want it to.
Blue to many will suggest a feeling of low
How about a magical healing presence
In your darkest need?
You feel you can't breathe, let alone come up for air
But something makes you surface.
Perhaps the energy of the healing blue?
It's how we see things through life
A free will to interpret.
The beautiful blue, vibrant in colour
Whether you choose to believe or not
Beautiful healing blue energy is everywhere.

Bold

It's time to stand up for one's self
To be bold
This isn't always a natural occurrence for you
But today or very soon one has to be heard
Your views and opinions are of great importance as
are
others
For some reason you feel yours aren't worth voicing
Why is this?
For your views and feelings are also of great import-
ance.
One might feel uncomfortable voicing your opinion
But stand bold you must
For the time we all have is so precious
A ticking of time
Not to be wasted by what ifs.
Everyone has a right to be heard
Not just those who like the sound of their own voices
But also the ones who don't like to be heard
For the silent person who watches from a distance
Often holds the keys to many doors
Including the chains one has often chained one's self to
So not to have to be noticed
Be bold, step forward and be heard
You will empower the others hidden away and en-

lighten
their souls
More importantly you will finally be free.

Both Sides

Flip the coin high in the air
Watch it land
Head or tails could land either way.
Oh, it landed on the wrong side
Does that mean the opposite view doesn't get no-
ticed?
Not allowed to be heard, bypassed?
There are always at least two sides to every tale
And every penny
Not every penny is a wrong 'un?

Bye Bye

Bye bye, it's time to say goodbye
So many feel uncomfortable saying these words
Goodbye!
How can this word have good in it?
I'll tell you why, because your paths will inevitably
meet
again.
Some even become weepy when saying goodbye to
family and friends
That often live in different areas or countries.
This is because the love is strong and one feels
connected
to another
We weren't designed to break our packs
As humans have evolved
We have learnt to think less of our pack and more of
our
individual needs.
It doesn't mean we care or love less
It's just the way we believe to be acceptable.
You wouldn't think of taking a wolf from a pack or
segregating half?
What of the psychological impact on the poor ani-
mals,
surely this would be Considered animal cruelty?

So funny us humans
Thinking as time goes on how we can self-sabotage
Not only do we farm out our young
But divide our pack
Thought provoking?

Calendar

A calendar for the year, a new diary for another new
year
What do we do at the end of the year?
We throw them all away
Stop!
Before you throw away take time to glance
Look at all the events and occurrences through-
out
the year
You have done so much?
Or perhaps very little?
Whatever you have done take a look, think
What would I like to do this New Year?
Maybe slow down a bit or quicken up?
Whatever you want for the coming year make it
happen
The pages of the calendar keep turning as so does
life
Such little time, spend it wise.
Let the pages keep turning out of control
Or ask why you are here and what your role is.
The choice is yours as it always has been
But remember one thing
This is your time on earth however you choose
But perhaps you could spend a day or two

Helping a few?

Cancer

Cancer such a terrifying word
For many the word has turned into reality.
A world all of a sudden turned upside down
Grief, fear, anxiety, anger and reflection.
A world once consisted of no time to stop
Now you are forced to stop.
A watching of heartache and despair filter through to so
many.
A loss of control and a feeling of helplessness
Reverting back to childhood
Exposing hidden wounds
All these emotions surfacing and spiralling out of control.
As the process and acceptance develops
So does the quiet tremble inside
For you are still alive
Now it's time to fight and grab life
Time stands still for no one
As occurrences throughout your life will evolve
Fight and survive
Or succumb and watch life go by
As life for all is a ticking of time.

Care

I care about our land and our lack of fresh air
I worry about the climate change and global warming.
I care about the safety of our young
Where will they be housed and who will look after them
when I am gone?
Sometimes I say to others
Maybe I care too much
Why can't I just not care like so many others?
For those who don't care as much
Seem less stressed and not so bothered by the obstacles
upon their paths.
If one loses the art to care
One has become submerged in their path too much
Are missing the lessons upon their way
For without care there is not time to share.
Imagine a journey without a care to share
Wouldn't it be sad, lonely and unfulfilling?
For we all secretly desire another's opinion
Surely only if that person cares?
So you see how this writing has gone full circle
Those people who become self consumed and don't care
for our surroundings

Their opinions we don't care for and certainly aren't
Interested to share.

Celebrity

What does this word mean?
For all celebrity means is a person so many have heard of
or seen
Usually media driven and wealth generated
So many of our young hunger for wealth and opulence
Why is this?
Maybe not receiving enough time from loved ones
Or perhaps considered the norm
Funny how one would want their privacy sabotaged
Not happy to be just exposed to the harsh realities of life
But also the vultures
For vultures see from far distances and never give up until
they have their prey.

Some do not have a choice
For the importance of their gifts is imperative
A sacrifice of oneself to the vultures
To benefit and open the eyes to all
To heal the wounded whether that is through lyrics, music, art or by example
A passion from somewhere so deep inside there is no option but to be exposed

These are the celebrities of our time

The people who care, share and most of all create light and hope.

So do you still want to be a celebrity?

Chapters

Chapters of life
Some mourn the end of each chapter
How about be thankful for each chapter.
Not all like change
But change is inevitable
As life and time stands still for no one.
Embrace each situation in life
For even the times of turmoil are priceless.
You here, living in the moment
Just now, this very moment
How are you?
Don't fret about the past
Don't worry about the future
Embrace this very special moment
A moment of silence, reflection
If you learn the art of this
Life becomes so much more enjoyable.

Cherish

Cherish everyone you meet upon your path
Don't question why they are there, just accept
Accept everyone you meet plays a part on your jour-
ney
If only to provoke thoughts and questions within.
Not everyone will share the same views and blatant
honesty as you
For in your world all is so simple
It's right or wrong, honourable or unkind
This is because you see the world and how it affects all
Especially the vulnerable
Not all will think of the weak and fragile
But just see the world from their prospective
It doesn't affect them and has no harsh impact on
their
loved ones and oneself
Then there is no problem, surely?
This is the view of the partially sighted
For it takes the full sighted to see and think of the
impact
on all
One can become irate with the lack of thought another
has
You mustn't for this is not out of malice
But naivety

A naivety to look past their present surroundings

Unable to dig a little deeper into another's world
Perhaps a world not as rosy as theirs

Cherish your eyes, use them well to notice all and beyond.

Children

Children are our future
Never change the person within
For we are all unique.
Some are loud and self assured
Others quiet and wish to lay dorm.
Respect the children
For they are all one of a kind
To be loved and nurtured
So they can fulfil this precious time.
Accept them for who they are
And embrace all their sides
See the beauty in all their uniqueness
Try not to worry, if your child doesn't conform
For the world would be so dull
Without the array of our little suns.
The creativity and discoveries these unique children will
bring
If only allowed to be a little different
And exceptionally unique.
Never try to change the children.

Church

What does this word resemble to you?
For many a haven, somewhere so precious to escape
to
A place where you can gather your thoughts and sit in
silence.
To sit in silence for many is a privilege
A place where one is greeted with familiar faces and
warm
smiles
For so many a bolt hole
Would otherwise become submerged
Beneath the harsh waves of life
Precious to so many.
Unfortunately,to others this word resembles hypocri-
sies
Anger and hate, a feeling of guilt
For not quite meeting the demands of the scriptures.
A guilt installed from birth
Finally escaped from the building of the church
But the thoughts and beliefs impregnated deep
within.
How can the word 'church' mean and feel two com-
pletely
different thoughts and emotions?
As this has been discussed before

There will always be good and bad, light and dark, yin and
yang
These exist in us all

It just depends whose hands these energies are held in.
One must never judge another's beliefs
Must remain open to all
But one must never be ignorant or turn a blind eye
To the wounded innocent
Certainly not because of faith
Otherwise faith can no longer live on?

Clock

Tick tock, tick tock
Endless time
It often seems, some things seem to last forever
Boredom, monotony
As one moans the clock is still ticking
Tick tock, tick tock
The passing of time is inevitable and so are you
Once graced with youth and aspirations
Now consumed with boredom and a lack of fulfilment.
Once a strong, athletic race horse
Now a has been.
Tick tock
The clock is still ticking
What shall your life be?
A life of adventures and stories to tell
A life full of experiences and learnt wisdoms
Or
A life full of regrets
I wish I had of ....
I could have been............
Quick the clocks still ticking
Tick tock

Coming Out

Today my darkest fear was revealed to the world
I announced first to family and friends
I was made a little different to other men
I struggled to put into words how I felt
For there won't be enough words I knew of to describe
The turmoil and distress I had hidden inside.

As expected my family and friends were supportive
But I could see through the sounds coming from their
lips
A slight look of bemusement and a little
disappointment
I had finally done it, I had declared to my loved ones.
Through time and self nurture
I will learn to accept
That I was born a little different
And sent from above to fulfil my role on this land
To perhaps help another who is born similarly
But to know we are all unique
One perceives the world with such different eyes
We must learn to respect every view
But try not to hurt the vulnerable too.

Connection

Sometimes in life you will
Make and often feel a connection with another
Another of similar back ground or often worlds apart.
The connection is heartfelt
Almost as if you know one another
Perhaps you do?
It doesn't matter, it is the connection
The reunion of two souls, finally meeting again on their
paths.
As the saying goes
You meet for perhaps a season, a lifetime or a glance.
We are all connected souls
Just some hold dear an extra spark
That is acknowledged by another who also has that extra
spark within.
Never question the meeting of two
If it feels right
Let it unfold and see where the path takes you.

Control

Controlling another's thoughts, controlling their actions,
how they conform in life
Quite controlling don't you think?
Even disturbing when you put it down in ink.
Each soul is here to experience life on earth
So important to feel, sense and see for one's self
Otherwise how do you decide the rights and wrongs
Most importantly the grey bits?
Nothing in life is black and white
The freedom to see with an open mind
Judgment not to be clouded by others
If possible not to judge but reflect.
How much could we all learn through
Untainted views subjected upon us from birth?
A world where you could decide what you thought about
this amazing and beautiful world.
Control – self control and responsibility is a good thing
Control over another
I'm not sure?

Creativity

Creativity if not accessed and controlled
Can erupt in self destruction and too much passion.
Passion is needed throughout life
For without
One doesn't truly live, but simply exists.
Existing without inner belief, desire or spark becomes mundane
A mundane life results in self suppression and little self
worth.
All of the above instigated by a naturally born creative
soul.
Creativity must be set free
For life cannot be lived happily without
All humans and living species are here to learn
And learn you will
Whether that be a life of living
Or living a life.
To allow oneself creativity
Is freedom to live?

Dare To Be

Dare to be who you are
If you're quiet and sensitive and happy this way
Then remain.
If you have no desire to change
Feel content in every way
Then please don't change.
For to know who you are and what are your views
You are the chosen lucky few
I repeat don't change.
If all around is forcing you to be something foreign to you
Ask yourself
Am I happy?
If the answer is yes
Then dare to be who you are and never change.

Depleted Energy

Depleted energy a result of our times
If not careful will pass you by
A life full of exhaustion as one will not listen to one's
self
Another reality of our times.
One will listen to media, friends and all
But not give oneself a thought.
You must learn the art of asking yourself
The truth hidden within one's self
For the inner you is humble and kind
Will always stand by your side
Only words of honesty will be heard
If only you would silence your busy head.
Time to look at all around
Notice again the passing of time
Who surrounds you and who are your true friends?
For a true friend may take a little energy too
But always give back to you.
Again I repeat these words of advice
Ration your energy to others but always be kind
Time to look at all around including the people who
surround
Be honest and true to yourself
By this I mean go on ask yourself.

Devil

What does this word mean to you?

I'm summarising something dark and untoward

The devil is your greatest fear, an insecurity you have locked away

Perhaps for some a substance they have chained them

self

to

Unable to escape or so they think, as it has become part of

who

they think they are?

Self harming physically, emotionally, repeated cycles of

self sabotaging

If I hurt myself it's ok because I am worth very little

The lists go on, childhood demons hidden away

Too scared to release for what would another think?

And still the list goes on.

Historically the word Devil has been used to put fear into

others

If one doesn't conform or do as some scriptures imply you'll go to hell.

Nice!

Anyone who had an open mind would work out the divine

or God
Only works in light.
So much fear put upon one another by so called fellow humans
But I shall say one thing
Each and every one of you is free to choose
Will I remain tied in chains of fear, self loathing, anger and
despair
Or simply remove these chains?
For my hands and mind are free to choose
A life of self induced misery by oneself or worse listening
to another
Or a life of simplicity, a sense of lightness and living?

Dictionary

A book consisting of thousands of words
All to describe a language, very educational.
The words that roam freely off one's tongue
We are often unaware of the impact they have on another.
We all have such responsibility when sharing our words
For time and time again
Wounded children become wounded adults
As the words unkindly spoken are taken through life
Impregnated deep inside.
Each and every one of us consists of a dictionary
Sad words, anger, hatred and self loathing
But thankfully we have been taught by the kind and caring
Words of joy, happiness and laughter.
Which words will you go on to teach others?
Words of remorse or words of love?

Don't Sit In Silence

Open your eyes
Not just to your world but others around you.
Share your concerns
Occasionally be truthfully open
Guess what?
The other person becomes honestly open
A once hidden secret
Or perhaps even a medical concern
Is now out in the open.
Feel the relief
Another has listened
Perhaps understands or even going through the same
situation
Or has experienced it.
All through taking the risk of being open, truthful and
honest
Daring to be exposed and vulnerable.
A problem shared is a problem halved
One of the truest sayings.

Doubt

Doubt not for you know the truth
You feel it in your heart
What is coming soon?
Why do you doubt?
When privileged to views upon this world
For the gifted, chosen are few
So many don't listen to their inner self
Is this due to fear, fear of succeeding?
To so many to be rewarded for hard work is hard to accept
I will repeat, you will succeed
Succeed with grace and honour
Those who strive with passion and good intentions in their heart
Will succeed just wait and see.
Doubt you may for this is part of you
But once you have conquered you can no longer hide behind doubt
For doubt you no longer can
Listen to these words, go with the flow but don't doubt
As I repeat you will see.

Dream Catcher

Why would one want to catch one's dreams?
For surely inner dreams and desires should be dared to be
set free
Once a dream could become a reality
But will amount to wasted energy if contained
Even the unwanted dreams need to be set free
If nothing else to dissolve away, freeing the person from
the chains.
All dreams need to be set free
The positive dreams to perhaps feed and ignite the inner
dreams of others
Once a dream is shared or given permission to be a reality
It is out there for all to enjoy
Whether that be to inspire the dreams of others and share
the excitement and anticipation
Of a tangible reality.
Without an inner dream
Life would be mundane
Predictable and not as fulfilling
The innocence of a child is born with aspirations

Its whether that child is taught to self believe
Or encouraged to catch the dreams and hide them away.
Feelings and emotions suppressed

Cause nothing but distress
Allow all to dream.

Enjoy Life

Life is beautiful
Life can be kind
But life also teaches us what one must ride
For the bumps can hurt
The gravel can graze
But ultimately
You will ride the test of time.
The waves can be unpredictable
The current cruel
But the sunshine is mighty
Especially those who ride through
The storm.

Life is a rollercoaster
Often consists of anxiety that makes you feel sick
Then a mundane calm and unpredictable corner
But an excitement of anticipation
Enjoy life!

Enjoy

Enjoy this life you must
Otherwise what is the point?
Every obstacle that will come your way
Let's admit it; there will be quite a few.
Reflect each day and learn you must
For knowledge and wisdom is to be gained
There will be ups and downs
But this is something you eluded to.
A life without reflection, understanding and joy
Is one of little worth?
If nothing more is gained from this life
Then at least have fun, laugh and spread light to all.
We all become so focused and channelled by our views
Stop!
Enjoy as this is also a part of you
Never lose the ability to enjoy
Or your time here is void.

Express

Expression is a form of art
Almost like learning from a drama class
Stood as a tree might appear extreme.
But the escapism of the willowing branches
Just to be
Not to be expected
Not to be involved
For you have become my dear the tree
Stood silently.
You feel nothing because you have allowed yourself just
to be Stood there as a tree
For today for this moment in time
Reading this writing has opened your mind
The importance of art and creativity
To silence one's mind.

Family

For those who are fortunate enough to have one
You are blessed
A unity of acceptance and belonging.
Often the family will bicker and squabble
But deep down there is a love
A bonding, yes sibling rivalry
But a stronger connection
Love!
The love if not nurtured
Can hurt and become unkind
Wear you out emotionally and reduce you to a child.
If one opens one's eyes
You will see
A love of unity
So please I ask you to put family issues aside
And see the delights a family can provide.

Fear Not

When new horizons come your way
Fear not
For new opportunities are to occur
Fear not
All will become fast and furious, exciting too
Fear not
For all your secret desires and dreams are to become
reality
I ask you to fear not
You will cope with all with grace and calm
Because you have already seen this dream from afar.
You have worked relentlessly and dedicated your time
All alone waiting for this time.
I ask one thing from you
Always remain humble to all around
And keep those feet upon the ground.
People will come as they will go
But rest assure you'll stand tall
Although at times made to feel small.
Your training has grounded you to the earth
Focus your mind to new challenges
Remember these words I give to you
You cannot falter off your path.

Feeling Low

Feeling low

Everything is fine you feel you have nothing to moan about

But for some reason there is a feeling of dissatisfaction

within one's life

A feeling of simply treading water but in stagnate, murky

water

You become annoyed with yourself

For I have so much to be thankful for

But yet one feels sad, confused dare I say a little lost

Why is this?

Especially for the person who always hunts for the positive

in every situation.

Because you are tired

A busy head that works overtime analysing every situation

Forgetting the mind fatigues too

The mind is such a delicate flower

One that needs to be nurtured, fed and watered

Not to forget the glorious light

Go easy on yourself

Ride the moment; don't fight it by over compensating by

cheeriness
Accept these feelings of stagnation for what they are
Acknowledge how you are feeling
As we have said time and time again
Time stands still for no one
As scenario's change on a daily basis
Once you were stagnate, next your feet won't have time
to touch the ground
Accept your feelings, acknowledge them and then my dear
You are free to move into clearer waters.

Find Forgiveness In Your Heart

How does one find forgiveness in their heart for the loss of a loved one by another?
Through an inner knowing they will be united again
Not a belief taught from birth
For many who forgive have no religion
They have something more powerful, they just know
They know with certainty this is not it, for this is merely a
land to learn.
How lucky and truly amazing are these people
For they were born with such knowledge and wisdom.
One must never judge the non-believer of religion
For these are often the untainted children of our world
They see with clarity the rights and wrongs
For their minds are free to see all realities.
That's not to decry the religious believer but remember
faith or no faith
We are all equal.

Flower

You are my flower
That stands tall
Your roots are grounded to steady all.
Your petals are of many
One for each of us
Never faulting to individual us
You are mighty in full bloom
Also gentle throughout the storm
Courageous and fun when sheltering your young.
You stand with silent confidence within
And share that self assurance to us all
You're bold, beautiful and funny too
The most amazing flower I have ever seen
For there is not another in this world
You are my flower and closest friend
My mother,
Thank you

Focus

To achieve one's dream you must remain focused.
Some will say I achieved by chance
It was simply, good luck and fortune.
No, your focus was so strong
It was always going to happen
Your subconscious that is.
We decide before we are born
What we will become
Some will say a gift from God or the Divine
To share with others
Everything is entwined within
A path, a destiny, a bumpy road.
Never shun away from what apparently appears
Upon one's path
Roll with it, for it is how you approach the obstacles
And often huge hurdles
That you grow and develop from
Not the smooth paths.
These paths allow us to develop into the true us
The wise us with all that wisdom just stored within.
Never shun from opportunities in life
Especially if it could benefit many.

Food

Wonderful food of every kind
Spices and flavours from afar
Will fill the room with warmth and smell
Give permission for people to congregate
Will create a chitter chatter amongst all
For small talk is simple and costs nothing at all
To share the delicious food
Invokes words of kindness to each other
So important to spend this time together
Or
All of a sudden
We will lose the art of loving and caring for each other.
If just sat in silence
Then let it be, but spend time in silence at least
together
at tea
If nothing else this will teach our young
The importance to make time for each other
Also to have a little fun.

Freedom

Freedom
Let it go
Pent up anxieties
Feeling alone and different among the crowd.
Just for today
Let it all go
Silence your mind of turmoil's
Quiet your inner self
Relax your body.
No wonder so many suffer from so many aches and
pains
For we have lost the ability to relax.
Sleep is so precious
A time to escape from the hustle and bustle
So why do so many wake throughout the night?
Stiff jaws and necks in the morning
Only you, yes you
Can find the solution to learning the art of relaxation
If you master relaxation properly
You have become free.

Frustration

Frustration and anxiety
You know there is more to life than you are fulfilling
A nagging desire to push the boundaries
To explore beyond what you perceive to be your
boundaries
You comfort yourself with how lucky you are
All you have and almost talk yourself out of asking for
more
But this something nagging away is more than just
wanting
It's who you are
Why you are here.
Deny yourself as much as you want
But this desire is embedded within for the fire burns so
brightly
Your soul can't do anything less than shine through
Your frustrations will subside as will you
When the time is right.
That is no excuse to waste the precious time
But accept who you are and yourself-worth
For souls who shine so bright
Can't remain anonymous all of the time
Watch this space.

Fun

Fun, so much fun and enjoyment to be had and found everywhere.

Fun in the sun

Fun on a winter's day

It's how you perceive this life

To just how much fun will appear on your run

So enjoy, your day

For everything is a heartbeat away.

Life is for living

As fun is part of life

So enjoy, embrace, smile, scream, and shout

But for goodness sake have

Some fun.

Gallop Away

Gallop away as fast as you can
Feel the air upon your face
The wind in your hair
The elevation of freedom and escapism
Finally a freedom to explore this beautiful world
Without the constraints of others.
So why have you galloped away?
Perhaps unable to listen to the negativity anymore
The constant reminder of not feeling part of the pack
A lack of importance felt from others
Childhood memories buried so deep
But keep rearing their ugly heads.
Gallop away my dear as fast as you can
For the elevation of finally escaping won't last long.
Unfortunately, memories and low self worth will rise to
the surface
What can I do to relieve myself of these sad thoughts?
Forgive yourself for the wasted precious time spent
inwardly raging
Love who you are, for you are unique
Not everyone can understand or like everyone for we are
all different
Hold your head up high; take the knocks of every kind

But remember my dear you are beautiful, pure and unique.

The final challenge on your ride is to look from their side

As you learn the art of forgiveness

The heart will heal and you will be able to feel the real wind upon your face

For finally you will be free.

Garden

A secret haven, a delightful place
Often with so many happy memories.
A place of contentment
No outside elements, T.V., radio, internet
Just rural
Often maintained with pride,
Nurtured and loved
Wild flowers and herbs flourish also
Beautiful.
My garden, our garden
So much simplicity and enjoyment
A time allowed to reflect
A place where feelings and emotions can roam.
No one else but you and the humble bumble bee,
If you wish.
Such a special place
A sacred space
All it requires is permission from you to enjoy
My beautiful garden.

Gone Forever

The grief so strong
Physically emptying the soul
The hurt so unbearable one hides away from all.
I can't control my crying
Let alone leave the house
For I am so scared I will crumble without you by my side.
I feel so alone
For this hurt and turmoil inside
Won't go away, won't subside.
What do I do, where do I go?
I have to continue for the sake of others.
So many depend on me
I need to take control, but I've lost control
This emotion and hurt inside is overpowering
As I curl into a ball and shut out the world
I embrace this moment by myself.
I feel something close
I can't identify
A presence of something close by my side.
That closeness of another
Lifts my head up high
As I gather myself together and step outside.
The world is a blur
The pain hidden deep within

But something or someone
Is giving to me
The strength to carry on.

Graffiti On The Wall

When one sees graffiti on the wall what does one think?

Some will see creativity, individualism and artistry

An inner flame of an exceptionally gifted person who sees

the world

With intriguing vision and emotional connection.

Who are all these up and coming artists?

How will we find out who they are?

We must get more of this elaborate work.

I need to understand more of the person behind this creativity

Why are they hiding who they are?

Taking risks to express themselves but remaining behind

hidden doors

Often a lack of self belief but a compulsion to do what is

so natural

Truly talented for you can't manufacture a born talent.

Such beauty the graffiti on the walls

I'm not talking about the anger and hurt of the wounded

children

Who vandalise through hatred, self loathing and despair

No, I am talking of the real artist who creates graffiti
on

the walls.

Guardian Angel

From the moment you are born
To the final moment you are here
You are never alone
For I am here
Your Guardian Angel.

A thought away
A worry or concern
Always shared for I am here.

So many say
I can't see my guardian angel
I reply
You don't have to
As I have said
I'm just a thought away.

Ask for help
You must
You will receive
If honourable and will be helped on your travels.

Unfortunately in life
Life can become hard, almost unbearable at times
But remember one thing
You are never alone
So walk the path

With silent confidence
As I have said
Just a thought away.

Heaven Has A Plan For You

You were born to make a difference
A difference you will make
You will leave a mark on this planet
One of energy and love.
The hearts and souls you have already touched are
many
So unaware of yourself and how you affect the emo-
tions
of others
Leaving a flicker of light in another
Whether it is in their thoughts or feelings.
You walk this path alive, shining bright leaving a trail
of
light
For all to enjoy, absorb and energise from
Such a selfless act to offer your energy to others
Especially the vulnerable and weak.
When times become hard and you feel you're losing
your
way
Remember not to worry
For heaven has a plan for you.

Holly Bush

The holly bush reminds so many of Christmas
A prickly bush
Like so many, hard to get to know.
Look a little closer
Look at the leaves
Although prickly on the edges, also smooth and gentle
in
the middle.
People are like holly bushes
They give off the exterior they want you to see.
But inside is a different story.
So many stories hidden away
Childhood memories, often issues, beliefs and funny
quirks.
The question is
Do you risk going near the prickly holly bush and
venture
into the middle?

Hope

Hope to hope all will be ok
I can see the light at the end of the tunnel
Just a little further
You can see it also, can't you?

So many can't see that flicker of light/hope
For life has been unbearable
The cards dealt unkindly.
I can't see
I can't breathe, my heart is beating out of control
I can't catch my breath.
Help!
Will somebody help?
Black, darkness – nothing.
Silence, nothing
For a moment
Peace, tranquillity, a glorious nothing
No turbulence, no fear, anxiety, sadness
Nothing, so quiet
Wake up, wake up
Suddenly the silence is broken
I'm back
The light is bright
Brighter than my eyes can tolerate
I'm back

Back in the land of hope.

Hush

Hush little one wipe away the tears
We see your anguish and feel your despair
Silence yourself
Feel, sense and know
We are everywhere
In your heart, in your mind and most certainly by your side.

Hush little one don't cry
For we are closer than one realises
By your side
We watch your hurt and wounded soul
You won't forget us
As you know
You worry day and night how you will cope on your own
But rest assure you most certainly will
For as we have already mentioned
It is impossible to walk your path alone.
These words are of comfort to all that read
One might feel lonely as you weep
But as I repeat
You are never alone.

I Can't Find
The Words

I can't find the words to say how sorry I am
Your pain and suffering I want to share
By this I mean just being there
I want to let you know
Whenever you need me, I will be there.
I have no words that can comfort you
But I can listen and care
That's if you dare.
It's safe to crumble by my side
For there will be no telling to other kinds
I just want you to know from my heart
I'm truly sorry.
Call me if you want to share.

I Feel Exposed

I feel exposed to all those who know
Know who I am and what's special about me
I stand by my conviction as I know I speak the truth
Although perhaps it may upset the few.
A few will be offended for one can't please all
Although not the intention I am here to benefit all
All one needs is an open mind
To accept these topics are a testament to time
Purity, light and love to all
Not to forget the healing energy upon the dawn.
For so many will read these words
And closure to issues will occur
Freedom to see the world once again
But without the heartache hidden inside
Feelings of lightness as your emotions are free
You are now free to be whoever you want to be
The real you.

I Love You

I more than care and want the best for you
I love you.
I feel your pain, your stresses and strains
I want to make them all go away, but I can't
For this is your journey
Which I have chosen to share
But I have to respect
Your decisions and just be there.

When you love another you must allow them freedom
A freedom to roam and self discover
By this I don't mean another lover
Watch, guide if asked
Never try to change the person
For this is the one you have chosen to share
Share the ups; share the downs but most of all care.
Oh yes, I forgot to mention
I love you.

I'm Bleeding

My heart is bleeding
Weeping tears of blood
The energy draining from my body
Not knowing how to stop.
Can't stop the anguish and unbearable hurt held inside
Afraid to speak
Too afraid to cry.
I need to let go for this hurt is eating me alive
Ruining my ability to function in the great outside.
How do I stop this bleeding and dreadful hurt inside?
For I know mentally how to carry on
But my heart won't stop bleeding inside.
Time for that plaster
Time to re-evaluate my life
Walk away or perhaps just die.
My soul is so bright
My mind alive
Please help me sort out this hurt inside.
Time to cry, let the tears free from your eyes
Then the bleeding heart will heal
And there's no need to die.
Now let that heart pump strongly
For the heart will heal
And so can you.

In The Arms Of The Angels

In the arms of the angels
They are everywhere
By your side, morning and night
Whilst in turmoil
They feel your tremble
They feel everything in the air.
For you are energy as are they
For energy is present within the two worlds
Just depends which side you are looking on.
Trust my dear the two will meet.
For the chosen few
Who are often ridiculed?
They see the two worlds in perfect unison
A burden at first to have these gifts
But once accepted and understood
A privilege and honour to do good
For these chosen few have been given the responsibil-
ity
to share
To open the minds of the sceptics out there.
A time will come when all will be proven
But until that time
Love and light must be given.

Joy

When joy comes your way, embrace
Really feel the excitement and fun within
Embrace that carefree sensation
Roll with it
Don't think, analyse or question
Just enjoy.
Situations change throughout life
One moment you feel content
Another time apprehensive
Look at the concern
What will you enjoy?
What anxiety can you turn into pleasure?
There is always a ying and yang in everything
Embrace every situation
For time is of the essence
As the essence is part of you.
So be joyous and when happiness comes your way
Which it will
Feel, absorb and embrace
Nothing more, nothing less
Enjoy.

Keys

So many keys to so many different doors
Will one take the risk and open the door
Or perhaps delay a little?
Delay as much as you want
For some doors will be opened
Often when not expecting and you haven't quite
Prepared yourself for the eventualities.
Some doors you will want to shut, close, lock and double
bolt
But first you must look at what you are locking away
For they have a nasty habit of appearing again
If you have dealt with the process and handled it well
Then you can close that door and all is well
For that door if processed and nurtured through, will remain closed
And you can move onto new.
Remember one thing; you are the game keeper with all
the keys.
Some doors will open without choice
But you have the final say which ones remain.

Kindness

The passer by who will risk his life
The friendly person who will open the door
The comforting expression from a total stranger
That says I've been there and understand.
Kindness truly still exists amongst so many
Just not always noticed
For those who are regularly kind and considerate,
Never change
For once in a while your kind gestures will be
acknowledged by the passer-by
And will be valued, will even invoke a thought.
How kind of that person
That was really nice
Somebody did something kind for me
Yes for me
That made me feel special and noticed.
I'm going to do that for another
They noticed
Gosh they said, thank you
Not so bad this thinking of others.
Always be kind
It's still there in society
You just have to look a little harder.

Laughter

Always make time for laughter
The most precious gift of all
Enjoying another's wonderful energy and lifting the
spirits of all.
What might appear ridiculously mundane?
Can make you erupt into laughter
When analysed on a sunny day.
We all perceive the world so differently
Through an array
So stop, talk, analyse and laugh on a rainy day.

It's how you tell a story
That can light up a room
So please don't ever stop being different
Always be you.
For you are a light worker
Who was put on our planet to work
To work for the hearts and souls of many
If just to make giggle.
The giggle inside warms the soul
And lifts the spirit so high
So go on continue
To make a difference and lift the spirits of all.

Lavender

Sweet smelling lavender
Pleasant on one's nose and kind on the eye
A haven for the humble bumble bee and a gentle friend to
Mother Nature.
A magical plant
Can aid sleep, heal wounds and relax the mind
Has been used by many throughout our time
So why oh why do I not see the humble bumble bee?
Where has he gone, why oh why?
Oh yes
Because of mankind.
Think before you extinguish anymore
Of Mother Nature's allies.

Life Is A Game

Life is a game, almost like a game of chess
Will you survive the storms or get knocked over?
Time and time one might fall
But nobody said how many times you could pick
yourself
up.
For those often who receive the most knocks
Become king and queen of their destiny.
It takes a brave soul to learn from their mistakes
Usually consists of heartache
For these people who grab life and continue their
journey
Are life's warriors and teachers.
These people are valuable and kind for they teach by
example
Often dedicating their time
Unaware how precious these strong people are
But most definitely admired from afar.
Will you be the pawn who remains fallen or a knight
who
rides through?
If you are willing to share your difficult times
Show there is always a way as light streams through
For it is impossible for it not to
Then you really have become the king or queen.

Life Is What You Make It

It seems too many, one unfortunate occurrence occurs after another
What about the in betweens?
There are so many beautiful heartfelt moments in between.
Just not always acknowledged
Often noticed briefly and not with appreciation
Simple things
A Child's warm smile
A hug meant from the heart
A longing from another desperately trying to ease your
load.
How amazing and lucky are you?
Surrounded by many who wish you nothing but good fortune.
I summarise, perhaps you did notice
But didn't allow the time to embrace.
Embrace you must for so much beauty and kindness
Really does go unnoticed.
For you are noticed
Now it's time for you to notice not just what's in front of

you
But all around.

Lighten Up

Does it really matter?
Such small occurrences that become massive issues
Anger, anxiety, ill health
All created by something so small
That began to roll
Collected moss, dirt and debris
Eventually became so big
It rolled on top of you
Crushing your chest
Making it hard for you to breathe
Unable to cope with the demands of life.
Why?
Did it really matter?
Choose carefully in life the things that truly matter
Let the others go
Allow yourself the gift of breathing freely.

Listen To Your Body

Listen to your body
What does it say?
How does it feel?
Perhaps tired, aches and pains created within
For some you will be unable to relax the body
You notice your jaw is tight
You have forgotten the ability to relax
Let the body flow.
Oh dear!
Time to notice the body and what it is saying
Unless you're going to let it break
For it is impossible to tense the muscles for too long a period
Otherwise they will soon not know what is normal.
Feel your body and all the aches and pains
Now try breathing slowly and relaxing the body
That's if one can still remember
Quite a shock for those who try
A reality check of our times
You hadn't realised the pressure you had held within
A body held so tight so not to crumble.
Listen you must to these words
Your body is telling you to stop and stare

Ease the tension upon yourself

If just to sit in the silence and breathe away the tensions

Stored within your shell

For rest assure my dear the anxiety and pressure one holds.

To you, you might be unaware

But please listen to your body

For your body will not deny

The pressure time bomb, from your eye.

Listen

Today you must listen
Listen to what another has to tell you
Don't interrupt, just listen
Really listen to what the other wishes to tell you
Remain non-judgemental, pass no view, just listen.
When the time is right and if they ask for your opinion
Remember all they have said
Perhaps feel the sadness, confusion and worry they hold
deep within
What is it they feel they should do?
Are they too confused to make the right decision?
Do they need a little more time to reflect?
What is the best for that person?
Maybe our views are ours and don't belong in their journey?
Sometimes giving permission to another to step out of
their situation
To be gentle and kind to themself
Reassurance everything will work out how it is supposed
to
Is enough
Not to taint another's decision but just to listen.

Look Through
The Window

Look out of the window
What does one see?
For some such beauty and luscious blues and greens.
We can all look out of our windows
The brave are the ones that step outside
Look beyond
The glass and blinds sheltering their eyes.
Once outside
You may feel vulnerable and weak
For all of you are now exposed to the harsh world.
Look, listen and feel
For you are truly alive
Explore the mountains that surround you of every
kind.
The mountains often steep
Will make your heart beat
But the satisfaction within, breathtaking.
So what has one learnt?
There is always a choice
Sit and watch protected by the glass
Or venture into the wilderness?

Love Life

Love life and life will love you back
Look at those who embrace life
Surrounded by light minded people
Their life containing laughter and fun
Why is this?
Again my dear, the law of nature
To always see a positive that once appeared as a
negative
Is learning
For those who think like this still experience the hurt
and
upset
But prefer to feel, learn and move on.
A wonderful way to be
For they have learnt somewhere along their path
The importance of time
How significant it is to ride the storms
As well as the good times.

Love The Outdoors

Love the wind upon your face
The gentle breeze upon your skin
The sensations of Mother Nature
Wrap up warm by all means but don't become a prisoner
indoors
Stepping from one building to another and then into another false environment the car.
Feel the crispness of the temperature
How does it feel?
Perhaps cold, even invigorating, harsh
You may not like the extremes of weather
Might make you feel uncomfortable
Make your fingers and toes hurt, you might even become
damp
Due to the rain.
If you hide from these experiences called nature
How are you to enjoy the warmth?
The shelter from the rain
The dry clothes upon your back
A world if one doesn't venture outside becomes complacent, lazy and low
A lack of appreciation of life.
Well maybe an appreciation of the confinement of

different four walls

To get the most out of your time on this beautiful earth

Yes beautiful if one looks

You need to take a risk and step outdoors

Thought provoking, how much time do you spend outdoors?

Memories

Memories so special and valued
Often one might stop in one's tracks and reminisce.
Might even bring a smile to ones face or chuckle
Happy memories fill us with warmth and contentment
To be stored and treasured deep within
For you have the ability to visit
Your own personal library whenever you wish.
As for sad memories
Look at the wisdom you have gained
The strength you took from the experience
And how you continued through your journey.
Often folk, years down the line
Will say they are thankful for one's times of despair
Not all
But most
For those who haven't yet
It simply means you have a little further to go
That's all.

Mental Dis-Ease

So much mental dis-ease among you folk
Why is this, I hear so many cry?
A world consisting of so much
Shelter, food, clothing so much.
War torn countries, natural disasters, poverty beyond
belief
Yet these countries have less mental dis-ease.
How can this be?
They tend to suffer in packs
Part of communities
Larger families and often, not always same beliefs
and
values.
What is so important in the Western world doesn't
exist or
is not a priority or concern.
It's often more important to feed the mouths of the
young
Or the sick and dying.
To provide shelter out of the blazing sun or shelter
from
the harsh winds
Overcome with crippling grief, a grief so unbearable
the
screams become silent

For the pain can't escape for fear of relieving would send
Shock waves across the land.
So why have us westerners lost the ability to cope mentally?
Have you not been listening?
Because one has become self-consumed
By materialism and lost the ability to think as a pack.
The art of sharing feelings, deep emotions and listening
to another.
Humans weren't intended to break free on their own
Back to basics, human integrity.

Mighty

The mighty have to fall

Without failure and heartache the warrior can't explore

The warrior who fights all the diversity upon one's path

The down trodden remarks

The envious eyes from afar

Unable to see the struggle of despair

Only able to see from the glare

Too consumed with what another appears to possess

Not interested in delving deeper to acknowledge the often self sacrifice of continuous mess.

The mighty fall, but pick themselves up

Focused on the task ahead

Not worried what materialism another has

For their desire to succeed is strong.

That's why the mighty have to fall

For occasionally to notice all

You cannot be mighty in this world and the next

Unless you credit all

That is the true mighty warrior who can reflect and see all.

Minds

Minds can be so fragile
The world is such a busy place
Rushing here, rushing there, and rushing everywhere.
A list for this, a list for that
No time to stop and reflect.
Stop!
What's the point if you haven't the time to stop?
Very little
For time travels by so quickly
So does youth and the body
The body quickly withers with time.
If you allow, you'll miss this precious time
All the teachings, experiences and adventures
What a waste of time
To be given such an amazing body/shell
To access all of the above
But to waste it on rushing and buzzing
From leaf to leaf like an excitable insect
Collecting pollen, what for?
The children have left
The grandparents old
What was it all for?

Money

Money, money, money
In the rich man's world
A world of power
A world of plenty
A world that what one wants one can buy with money.
Yachts, fast cars, luxury holidays with breathtaking views.
Money, how wonderful money can be?
Then one becomes ill
Money can buy the best treatments
Care and medication.
What do you mean you can't do anything?
I'll pay to fix it
Yes that's what I'll do.
The time has come
Money can't buy everything
Time to enjoy the simplicity of life
Each other
The silence of the ticking clock
The touch of the other's hand
The bond between two souls who are entwined
Beautiful.
How did I not notice?
The most precious belonging I had
Right in front of our eyes every day.

Only the foolish are blinded by wealth
It's how clever you are with it
Not to become it.

Names

Most are born and given a name
A name, what does this really mean?
The name whether it be a mundane or eccentric name
Doesn't make the person all of a sudden become a
conformist or outrageous?
No
The person brings the name to life
The person makes the mundane name mischievous,
fun
loving and carefree or
Makes the eccentric name quiet and reflective.
Funny how we name one another
Funnier still how we label our young at such an early
age
Not even giving them time to develop and grow into
whoever they want to be.
A sad reflection of our society
Having to conform and behave in an acceptable way
like
everyone else.
I say the world needs the slightly eccentric
Desperately needs the nurturer
Not to forget the warriors
Otherwise wouldn't one's journey be rather boring
If we never had the chance to walk our paths with such

variety?

Never Doubt

Never doubt you have a purpose in life
For you are unique
Very special
You might be unaware of this but it is so apparent to others.
Focus your energy
Find the calm within
We all possess all the different tools needed to get through
one situation to another.
Never doubt
Who you are
What you represent and that wonderful light within
As I've already said
You are unique, beautiful and held dear to so many.
I'm not talking of another
As you might shudder with these humbling and kind words
These words were meant for
You!
Never doubt, always believe
As so many around you do.

Never Hurt Another

For you know what is right
No excuses to hurt another.
For those who hurt will be shown the error of their ways
As we all will.
If you know your behaviour or words will hurt another
You have no right
To inflict hurt and anguish onto another.
It is their right to choose
As you also have a choice
But don't play victim to another
For you have become that person's
Achilles heel.
Take the hit, turn your cheek
But don't succumb to hurting another
For all you are doing is invoking unpleasantness
Which in turn will come back
As this is the universal law

On My Own

Today I have the luxury to spend time on my own
I sit quietly, restlessly being alone
Why can't I enjoy this moment I ask myself?
For I should be working and doing my best
Sit still, relax let the tensions dissolve
For it's healthy and ok to do nothing.
Where has this guilt derived from?
Yourself!
Occasionally let yourself sit still
Do nothing and wallow in the silence
For this time to bathe will reignite your soul
Make you more hungry and passionate
For another day.

Open One's Eyes

Open your eyes to all around

Look at the innocent children with not a care in the world

Look again, so many of our young hold the worries upon

their shoulders

The guilt of eating the few remains left in the fridge

Listening to the adult assuring them they really aren't hungry

Knowing too well the loving carer is becoming ill due to

lack of fuel

Look a little closer

If prepared you will be faced with the truth

So many mouths going hungry

Not only in far away countries

But right in front of our eyes

Often unnoticed by the rush of time

For so many don't open their eyes

It's time to stop

See all around; notice the needy as well as the proud.

Open Your Eyes

Open your eyes
Not partially, wide
What can you see?
The telly, washing machine spinning around
Don't forget the laptop and tablet.
What can you see?
You see very little
So many see nothing but manmade gadgets
Imaginary fantasy friends on twitter
A world where one can be who they want
Hidden behind a screen.
Really!
So so wrong
Unhealthy and eerily warped
Time to get out in the elements
Yes, fresh air
You might notice
Our world is actually very beautiful
If one will stop and stare.
People are real
Visually and emotionally
Everyone needs to learn the art of connecting
Once again time to go back to basics
Before we destroy this as well.
Easier to hide behind that screen and interact

With virtual reality
Which will it be?
Imaginary world or the real world
Where humans and nature exist?

Open Your Heart
And Mind

Open your heart and mind to others
Whether that be their beliefs, notions or vulnerabil-
ities
Be open to others
Not to judge
Listen with interest and belief
It's not for us to judge
Be happy for them
That they believe in whatever it is that makes them
safe
and secure.
Better to feel safe in this world
Then insecure without one
That's for those who need to believe in something
For some it is simply a belonging
To be identified as one of many
Who are part of something.
When you see it like this it's not a bad thing really
A feeling of belonging
For those who believe in nothing
Some will be self assured and content
One must respect this.
Basically the foolish preach and dictate to others

The wise, listen, observe, support and don't judge.
That's the way we should all be
Open hearted and our minds alive
Anticipating others intellect, beliefs and passions
But remaining non-judgemental
That's the wise king of our times.

Our World

Our world what a beautiful place
The oceans roar with such freedom and grace
The sand grainy and golden upon the beach
What a wonderful place where we belong.
The greenery fresh crisp and alive
Allowing nature to roam by.
Untampered mountains from afar
Catch our imagination from our hearts
The insects and bugs so thought provoking too
There is so much to discover and to do.
Not to forget our furry friends
Fascinating how they see the world with such simplicity
Taking only what one needs
Our world consists of such beauty for all to see
If only one would look at the reality
As time is passing if not careful so will our beautiful world
As concrete mayhem is over developing
So how can one help this frightening reality?
Start with caring and at least recycling.

Pain And Suffering

There is so much pain and suffering throughout our world
So many live daily with excruciating physical pain
Often fuelled to the brink with concoctions of pain killers
Sadly so many unable to function without
Others dependant on manufactured pharmaceutical chemicals
Cocktails of pills and drugs
Too scared to reduce or go without.
Psychologically dependant for this is now who they are
They have been diagnosed; have even been given a name
Finally they fit into a condition
Have been labelled and put in a box.
When the person needed help and support
Often human contact and time
There was no time
The medication was a quick fix to get them out the door
A conveyer belt of suffering people
The pills became their crutch
That enabled them to carry on
But deep down the longing for help and support was bubbling within

The problems and cause of pain still undetected
But has a name
So go on then take the array
Of pills
NEXT PATIENT PLEASE!

Paranormal

Paranormal is a funny word

Simply means a strange occurrence to some, that can't

quite be explained.

This word often induces fear and dark thoughts

Especially to the less opened minds

Usually fragile minds that have been tampered with

Have lost the ability to think for one's self

Not daring to question the scriptures for they would surely be punished?

Thank goodness for the intellects, the scientists, the free

spirits and most important

The untampered minds

For paranormal has and always will exist

For so much is yet to be discovered throughout time

A beauty beyond belief

Scope for self-discovery

And wondrous healing energies

All to be discovered by open minds with time

For closed minds might choose to resist

But unexplainable occurrences are evolving all the time

Better to be part of and create light

Then hide beside fear.

Peace In Your Heart

Today you made peace with the world
More important you made peace with yourself
You opened your darkest fears aloud
They were finally listened to and understood
It took real courage to voice your fears
It also took great strength for the other person's ears
One to talk from the heart the other to listen from afar.
Communication is the key
The key to the door to venture more
New adventures to come your way but now one can see
past the rainy days.
Always be honest to those who care
But you must remember to always be there
Communication is a two way thing
To speak aloud of your concerns
But always to listen in return.

Peace

So powerful this statement
Perfect peace is a gift.
To find inner peace and self-acceptance is an honour
For very few master this.
Some whilst lying on their death bed
Still fighting self-acceptance and the magical peace.
Peace with others, peace with this life
Most important a peace with yourself.
So I hear the thoughts of many
How do I learn peace?
By embracing every moment of every day
The good, the bad, the indifference
Knowing you have contributed a loving light energy
To the best of your ability to all
That creates peace.

Pick Yourself Up

The ability to pick one's self up is of paramount
For what other option is there?
An existence of just being
Not even acknowledging the beauty of the breath
To be alive
Your time here is so short and valuable
A time to learn and experience
If nothing else the wind, rain and warmth upon one's
face
You will learn what is put upon your path one way of
other
It just depends on how much input you want to add to
the
situation
For experiences are inevitable on your journey
It's how you choose to deal with them that is the
learning
Conquer inner fears and desires or become consumed
and
suppressed
All these decisions all on your path
Nobody else to blame, for this is your journey
Pick yourself up, brush yourself down and if nothing
else
Let the journey begin.

Pictures

Pictures are priceless
Pictures to share
Pictures to nurture
Pictures taken to show you care.
Thousands of memories stored within
An art gallery and museum
All in the air.
In your heart, mind and soul
We store so many pictures
And in time
Once again we will share.

Poppy

The beautiful, passionate and strikingly breathtaking poppy.
The poppy resembles times of sadness
But also strength, determination and a desire to succeed.
The poppy, one often describes historically as the flower
of death
Look a little closer
It also resembles new life
A continuation of life upon so many
Who went on to procreate and spread the tale of
heartache and destruction
And how humans mustn't behave in such barbaric ways.
To spread the seeds of the poppy
To spread light and love to all
And to teach the young that nothing comes from
spreading darkness
Yes one must acknowledge
But not re-enact
For light cannot be contained
And like the seeds of the poppies
Light also must spread freely
Amongst the fields.

Precious Love

Love like you have never loved before
Embrace every minute of every hour
For love you must
Feel the air upon your face
Watch the leaves change colour upon the trees
Notice the colour and diversity of our skies
Embrace it all.
For those who are fortunate to make old age
You have the luxury to reflect on one's life
No regrets of any kind
As you can look back and reminisce
For you have loved with all your heart
Including the ticking of time
A celebration of life of every kind
Well done.

Pressure

So much pressure
Pressure to multi-task and to conform
We hear so often one say to another
What are you doing today?
Pressure, often self induced
Can't appear lazy, must be striving forward and filling
the
day
Often with meaningless tasks.
Halt!
Slow down, the work can still get done
Just perhaps with a little less anxiety.
So many not enjoying the presence
Striving to complete and move onto the next task
Pressure!
Who's inducing and creating all this pressure?
Maybe a little from one's self?
Learn to enjoy the pressures in this world
By eliminating the physical anxiety
Or
Become like an old fashion kettle
Whistle, scream and shout at those you love
And eventually boil over.
Time to reflect the self induced pressure?

Quiet Your Mind

Chitter chatter, chitter chatter
Your minds buzzing all the time
Hardly allowing one to process the mind
Analysing this, analysing that
The chitter chatter goes on.
Goes on inside your head
Emotions, despair, worry and concerns
Often amounting to nothing
But still I hear the chitter chatter
Time to STOP!
One thing at a time
Think have your thought
Then move on
One thing, as one day at a time.
So much mental dis-ease amongst so many
Silence the chitter chatter within
Allow yourself to think.

Rainbow

Red, yellow, pink and green
Purple, orange and blue
I can see a rainbow
See a rainbow too.
You must listen with your eyes
Listen to how you feel
Listen to how Mother Nature feels too
For I can see a rainbow
See a rainbow too.

Energies array in a multi-tude of colours
Infiltrating our world and beyond
A sombre mood of self loathing
Infiltrated with positive colours of an amazing
arrangement
So listen, look and feel for that rainbow
And you will see the rainbow too.

Relax

Yes certain things have to be done today
But what about the other things, worries, concerns
clogging your mind?
Focus your thoughts on what truly matters
The health of your mind
Your minds are so precious for this creates the actions
you
do
How many times have we heard stories of erratic
behaviour?
Resulting in hurting of others and one's self
Sad, really sad.
For that person didn't allow themself the time to focus
On what is really important
Your views, feelings and thoughts are so important
Not the views of others
But yours
Within every person is a pure beautiful light energy
So unique and full of beautiful love
A love so pure it can only create light to others
The true person
How about silencing the mind, delving a little deeper
And finding the real you
Not the child who uses excuses of I didn't know better
and

blaming others
But taking control of yourself
Your untainted, true self
Wouldn't that be amazing?
It is completely up to you.

Respect

Respect one must, of all around
The different cultures and shades of every kind.
Respect we are all different
And see the world though different eyes
It's so important to keep our minds alive.
We must learn from one another different sides
But most of all look and respect
What each individual holds inside
For all are unique.
That bright soul that is naked to the eye
Sense, feel and watch if that person is kind.
All consist of light within
Some shine brighter still
Allowing freedom to share that pure energy within.
These are the ones to respect the most
For a selfless act to share amongst most.
It is easy to respect those who are easy to respect
But one must learn the art of respecting the often
unrespectable
Who do not care
One must respect all energies out there.

Rest

Rest your weary head
Stop the thoughts spiralling around in one's head
Rest your body too
Be aware of the tension you hold in your neck
The jaw is tight the arms too
Shocking as noticed by so few.
Clear your head of whirling thoughts
Just for the moment close the doors
Sit in the silence if one must
To catch your breath and hear your thoughts
Not someone else's from afar
But the true person inside, that bright shining star.
You will answer all concerns if only given the opportunity
That honest vibrant energy you hide inside
Who only knows words of truth
So all you have to do is quite simple
Ask yourself what to do.

Ride The Storm

Funny how life can unravel
One moment life is running along smoothly
Then all of a sudden a catastrophe appears
Well we didn't see that one coming.
Life can be so unfair
Yes
Life can be cruel but also magical.
So many wonderful occurrences are taking place or just
about to
For every unpleasant situation
There are more positive.
When life becomes hard
Remember these words
Everything evolves, time stands still for no one
Sad times will pass as new horizons occur each day
A ticking of time that will pass away
Embrace and ride the storm
For as we all know
After a storm, comes light and then
The glorious rainbow.

Robin

The Robin
Such an attractive looking bird
With their bold red breast, quite eye catching
One might even relate this bird to Christmas.
Treasure the robin
For they are becoming few
When was the last time you saw a robin?
A time many a year ago
You would see rather many
We tend to see more pigeons, magpies and crows
Why is this?
They have adapted to our society
Have more scavenger tendencies
Will steal from one another
Even prey on the young of others.
A bit like our society?
Many will say this has always happened
Yes I have to agree
But now, man has made it even easier throughout the
internet
For our young to be preyed upon
This is a huge concern
But not for one to become scared
Just a realisation for the parents
To stop and stare

Open your eyes and be aware.

Roots

You can't change the roots you come from
As this is part of your history
One perhaps your children will go onto study
Stand proud of who you are however controversial your
family history is
For yes you were born into this family tree
But as a bud you choose to flower into whatever your
heart desires
For with water, light, clean air and most important
love
If not from those family branches around you then
from
yourself
You can change history
The flower that spread her seeds to others
Shared among the weak
Gave hope to the petals that had hit the ground
You gave them hope when all around was bleak
Simply by being you
The bud that flowered and escaped tradition.

Rushing

Rushing here, rushing there, rushing everywhere
Why so much rushing
For surely if one rushes all the time
One will miss the moment
What it might have resembled
What you might have heard, noticed and learnt
So why the rush?
So many miss the passing of time
The innocence of the developing child and ageing parent
Time my dear will stand still for no one
As the process of aging cannot be halted.
Each and every one of you will live a life
For how long, no one can answer that
Maybe to old age, perhaps one will be short changed
But no one knows
Continue to rush if you must
But don't look back with regrets
As once mentioned, time stands still for no one.

Sea

Look at the beautiful views of the sea
Just look at it
Miles upon miles of sea
Nothing else just an array of blues, greens and greys
You might notice some birds
Listen.
Nothing else just the sea, something so calming and
relaxing simply looking at the sea
Listening is so captivating.
Now smell, so salty but fresh
So natural and untampered with
Not a smell that has been manufactured to please
But left with simplicity.
How do you feel when left alone?
Just you and the ocean?
I'll tell you
Hungry and alive
Alive to carry on and embrace your surrounding
For like so many you become submerged
Almost drowning in society
But now you have risen to the surface and feel alive.
Make time for nature and Mother Nature will help
Calm your mind.

She Cried Wolf

She would cry wolf time and time
Until one day she cried no more
For her cries were many, some would say
Until that wondrous day.
Her body ached, she would feel sick
Repeatingly would go where she felt she would be
safe
The professionals ignored her cries for help
Until too late to save the day,
The lesson of this story is
A person really does know if they are sick
Always believe in yourself
And never stop asking for help
If you have a bee in your bonnet
That all is not right
Pass your concerns to many
For eventually you will find what is right.
For many it's so simple to cure
Time to be heard and someone to share your thoughts.

Silence

Silence is a gift from above
A feeling of nothingness
No thoughts running through your head
No worries or concerns of any kind
Silence!
Silence is beautiful and pure
Recharges your energy and ignites the soul.
Time to breathe, notice your breath
Nothing else present just you in your head
A lovely moment
Just you with your true self
The spirit so pure, gentle and soft
An innocent energy eager to please
Childlike with freedom to explore.
Bliss the silence and freedom within
Such a rarity and special moment to open the door
A door to self-discovery, the keys are all yours
Now which door will you open and venture
through?
For you have all the answers
If only you will silence yourself and just be.

So Kind

So kind, so many of such different kinds
Such loving people exist within our world
Precious souls sent from above
Who care so deeply about all of us.
They spread themselves far to you
Helping so many others in all they do.
Their words are uplifting in every sense
They will halve your worries inside your heads
They are warm, tender and make you feel safe
Always welcome and put time aside
For you are made to feel of great importance
Whatever the day
You are the kindest person I know and I want to say
With simplicity from my heart
How important you are and what a wonderful light you
share to all
Thank you.

So Much Worry

Worry over this, worry over that
Too much, too little
Good but not quite good enough
So much worry.
For many, you will spend a life time of worrying
Exhausting the art of worry
Especially the expert worriers
Did you ever think?
It really doesn't matter one way or another
For the destination is the same
Just one path full of exhaustion and unfortunately ill
health
The other path, one of enjoyment and embracement.
The journey is the school of life
The destination a time to reflect.
Seriously think about your vocation or path
Whatever you have chosen
Ask yourself
Do I want to enjoy this life or exhaust myself?
Pushing along to the final line?
Think, maybe a life of fulfilment and enjoyment
It's up to you?

Soldier

So many lives lost through pointless wars.
Not to the soldiers who risk their lives to protect their homeland
Unfortunately many a soldier returns to the true homeland
before their time
Not fulfilling the passing of time
That's the sacrifice of our young men and women
Never decry the soldiers time for many are trapped financially in this time
Often escaped from a world of destruction and lack of compassion
Not knowing the true meaning of love.
I speak of few for all have a previous life before
Some desperate for adventure and escapism from mundane
But weren't quite expecting so many blood thirsty days.
Always look from both sides of the battle field
For all have a tall story to tell
Remember you must, these boys and girls
Have parents as well
Some with families watching from a far
So please don't judge, for one can't truly speak without

the experience of war.
Freedom of speech by all means
But judge not.

Stained Glass

Something so magical about the coloured glass
Beautiful and cheery
Notice the light as it filters through
Imagination able to run free alluding to you
Almost childlike the array of colours
Freedom of a rainbow ricocheting
Bathe in the colour enjoy and digest
As very rarely these days
We allow such vibrant colours our way.
Feed the world with more colour
Vibrant energies too
For such fun and creativity is to come to you.
A world of colour is beautiful to all
To share, create and spread to all.
So what am I saying throughout these words
Ingest, digest and so important to share
A little coloured light to all.

Starry

Starry, starry nights

Look up at night and look at all the breathtaking beautiful

stars.

Some brighter than others, but all unique

Some so far away

Barely visible to the eye

Bold stars pushing to the surface

You will always get the subtler star

Who sits by happy not to be noticed

And the stronger stars who will do anything to be noticed.

Why is this?

For often the shy, less apparent star will hide at the back

But what this star is yet to discover is

People like something or someone a little different

A different aspect to talk or think about.

We have already seen the bright stars

But are still hungry to discover

The unattainable stars hidden from afar

Rest assure with time, they will shine through

For a true star cannot go unnoticed.

Stork

The stork carries the new born baby within its' beak
The sound of tiny pitter patter of the baby's feet
New life what an amazing miracle
So much joy and relief finally the tiny person has safely
arrived
Life is so precious and limited by time
But there is no time on the other side
Time and time again we hear
I wish so and so was here, to see this new member of our
family
Do you not maybe think or feel they perhaps are?
A testing of time all will be revealed
But for now my dear
Embrace your child, shower in love
For there is no greater gift you can give to the new
A warm safe home, made by you
Show kindness and nurture
For they will grow up to give to others to
Remember each chapter goes by so quick
So love every minute of every hour
As time goes quick
Times will often be exhausting as well as fun
For your bundle of joy

Will most certainly keep you up morning, noon and night
Enjoy!

Strawberries
And Cream

A hot summer's day
Clear blue skies and summer's delight.
Not a care in the world
No responsibilities today
Just a day to relax on this gorgeous summer's day.
There is no routine
I'm not wearing a watch and I'm feeling completely at
ease
I sit on the grass
Feeling nature upon my feet
Feeling the blades of grass tickle my toes
I've never noticed the soil and textures before
A reflection I cannot ignore.
I've lived on this planet all of my life
And this is the first time
I have thought about life
What a wonderful planet, sky and all
I really must make time for all
How shallow and self centred I have become
That I truly never noticed the writings on the wall
When one hasn't exposed one's feet upon the grass
Never felt nature upon one's skin

What have I been doing not to notice such simpli-
city?
Today I will correct the error of my ways
Open my eyes with a different gaze
I will finally open my eyes
Including the delicacies exposed to all
The most precious things in life are free
Just allowing yourself time to be free
And occasionally eat strawberries and cream.

Struggling

Struggling with work
Struggling with your home life and the loved ones around
you.
I'm just struggling
Sit tight my loved one
For you are simply weathering the storms.
After the storm there will be calmness and sunshine
For all that is occurring, is growth.
Growth and development within
For nothing can stay the same
Otherwise life would be rather dull
What would you learn?
Very little
As a child hits their milestones so do you.
It doesn't stop after puberty
But continues throughout life.
So you're struggling?
Sit tight, weather the storms
Often feels worse, still too many
Here comes the calmness
You are evolving all the time, your views, thoughts
How you perceive all around.
Don't struggle, step back, observe
Who knows you might notice something

Something about you and an acceptance of another?

Study

To study is and can be so rewarding
But for many an obsession to study and achieve
Can become paramount.
Certificates of achievements
Which turn into self importance, status and class?
Very good, but now what will one do
With all these important pieces of paper?
Hopefully something of good
For the practitioner, we know can study
But now must show their worth by their results
Especially the teacher and medical examiner.
The art of listening and feeling what is right for the individual person.
Notice how I used the word person
Unfortunately books categorise symptoms and case studies.
People are unique and don't always fit into boxes
This is where the study begins
For not all have the ability to sense, feel and hear
What another has to say.
For this is a study of itself
One unfortunately doesn't receive a certificate of self importance
But through word of mouth
Will receive clients and reward.

Sunshine

You are my sunshine
The light of my life
When all around appears murky
Your light filters through
When times are hard and I don't want to carry on
Your array of sunlight always sees me through.

You're joyous and kind
I've never met anyone quite like you
For your tirelessly giving and receiving very few
Your energy so bright and cheery to
Oh how we need people like you.
You're more than just a friend who listens too
You're a life changer
Who constantly filters love through?
Always remain true to yourself and others
For without your sunlight this world wouldn't matter
Thank you.

Sweet Child

Sweet child of mine
I watched you grow by my side
I witnessed the moves and emotions of every kind
You brought so much joy, wit and laughter
But also anxiety and anger
You taught me more beyond belief
For there is no special manual to keep.

I love everything about my child
Although at times, very testing
My life is complete having you by my side
Shall never be parted
I repeat
Even when my shell dies.

Take A Break

Luscious greenery, snow drizzled mountains
Fresh air in our lungs, the wind upon your face
Just for that moment
Not a care in the world.
Holiday you must
For some don't put any value on the time to get away.
Get away whenever you can
For time out is of great importance
A time to reflect on life
What importance you are playing in this life
If it's a life of mundane
But you are feeding the mouths of the young
Then you have an important role
Be proud for feeding the mouths
Also don't forget to nurture the young and show them
The value of work.
Not to just work for one's self
But to work for many.
That is a role model of society
Teach but one must not preach.

Take Control

This is your time
Time to discover every kind
Situations and scenarios will come your way
But what one must remember is
There's always another day.

Each day is a fresh start
On how you want to be
A world of wonder and mystery
Please remember these words
For they are short and sweet
Today is you and you are today.

Television

A world of escapism
A moment in time where you can focus your attention
away from reality.
Can be an educational experience
Often thought provoking and enlightening if rationed
But unfortunately can create fear, anxiety and depression.
Escapism is healthy
Any dependency in any form to deal with life or hide from
reality
Can become an addiction.
How often do you sit in front of the T.V.?
Quite interesting
Time to reflect for life is for living
Not to be wasted sat in front of a box.

The Best

You all deserve the best
The best also deserves you.
So many accept very little for themselves
But desperately want the best for their loved ones.
How can you expect the best for others
Especially the young
When they see what little you expect for yourself?
Children learn by vision, vibrations and expectations
You too deserve the best
Can have the best
When you are willing to receive the best
For the best is YOU!

The Busy Bee

Watch the busy bee
Hard working and humble
Only takes as much pollen as he can carry.
Works so hard
Has a huge purpose
Shows the young, the values of nature.
Mustn't take too much
Mustn't destroy
Must get just the right balance
So not to tilt Mother Nature into self destruction
Create erratic cloud formation and global warming.
Life is a fine balance
A balance to be shared equally
Not to tip the scales
So all can enjoy.

The Heart

The heart the precious pump of the body
Not only does it pump blood to all the vital organs
But sends shock waves of emotions throughout one
Physiologically the powerhouse of our precious bodies
If the heart medically has a problem
It will literally stop one in their tracks.

What about a broken heart?
We hear time and time again
Two united souls that have spent a life time together
Die shortly one after another.
Why is this, for there is no scientific evidence to prove it?
Although many a humble open minded doctor will agree
The other patient died of a broken heart.

Our hearts push us on throughout this life
When pain and heartache becomes too much
Not only do we feel the pain of others
But our hearts weep too.
Look after your heart
Go gentle on yourself when times are hard
Always allow the heart time to heal
And in time so will you.

The Rainbow

Look at the beautiful colours
All merged into one
Like humans
A vibrant array of different energies
All mixed in the pot of treasure at the end.

All your energies, feelings and emotions all entwined
The life lovers giving so much more into the pot
Allowing their vibrant happy care free energy to infil-
trate
The less vibrant colours
Those who see life through half full glasses
Being made to see a little clearer
A little more fuller the wonderful life that surrounds
us.
What a beautiful array of colours
We all are
Helping each other along our paths
The beautiful rainbow.

The Swaying Of The Tree

Have you ever noticed the swaying of a tree?
Look closely how it bends from side to side
Almost looks like it's going to snap
But fortunately it doesn't
For if one snaps
You could hurt so many.
All the tiny branches hitting the innocent on the way down
Knocking one down after another
Catastrophic
All because one wasn't prepared to bend a little.
Like the branches on a swaying tree
You have to learn to weather the storms
Often having to bend
Not only to protect others but yourself also.
What is the alternative?
To shatter the lives of so many or maybe
Just go with it?

This Is Your Moment

This is your moment to shine
The here the now, your time
With destiny and desire the two can only meet if acted
upon
Sit and dream all day if you wish
But dreams need a little action
So don't waste anymore time
Just do it!
You have thought long and hard
Repeating these thoughts time and time again
Now just have a go
Finish off what you have started
Or begin
But waste no more time
For time on earth is so precious and consists of very
little
If it feels right, stirs emotions of excitement and you
truly
believe
Then go for it!

Time To Rest

Time to rest
One's weary head
Time to escape and drift off,
One must allow one's self the freedom to escape
For if not, one's health could be at stake.
Health is golden, sweet and pure
Taken for granted
Until one hits the floor.

Once the floor is hit
It awakens the soul
The head starts spinning
Again and again.
Now you're forced to acknowledge your health
Value the simplicity of life.
Health must be valued again and again
For unfortunately you humans
Don't and won't rest that weary head.

Learn from these words
If just for today
You can't keep burning the candle
Night and day.

To Be Joyous

Isn't it wonderful when one finds themself laughing out
of control?
You laugh so much your sides hurt
You struggle for breath
It's so enlightening
Lifts your whole body, mind and soul.
Just for those few moments
There is nothing else that matters to you.
Just the pleasure of pure laughter
Laughter is truly amazing, healing and a feeling of oneness
with yourself.
You can't learn laughter
For it's a natural occurrence
If you are a true light worker you will make others smile
and enlighten them
Perhaps not roar with laughter out of control
But lighten their load
Fill them with a sense of happiness and amusement.
These light workers are priceless
More valuable then they will ever know
For often not taken seriously and taken for granted.
If only you all knew the true value of the spirit lifter

One of the most valuable people on our planet.

To Receive

So many shudder at the thought of receiving
Much easier for the majority to give
One must learn the art of acceptance.
To accept is allowing the other to give
For those of you who are givers
Enjoy the whole experience
As it gives the person self worth, importance and a
purpose
I would go as far for some their identity.
Next time you turn down an offer of help, support or
kind
words
Remember you too are worthy to accept
As they are to give.

To Type

So many type, type away
Half the time unaware of what one types
Not really thinking what one is saying
Self absorbed in the moment
Not a care in the world
For what I type is how I feel
How I perceive the situation
What I believe to be right.
Happy one continues to type away
Oblivious to the world
For at that moment all that consists is their world
One of great self importance
And one where everyone will finally listen
To ME!
The typing floats out into the sky
For thousands to see and read
Upsets many, hurts and angers too
All these negative feelings created by
The self importance of ME!

Today I Heard
You Were Ill

Today my friend confided in me
He told me of his worry
A serious health problem
I didn't know what to say
For no words could cure him
I simply listened
As he spoke of his hurt
I felt his pain
As he spoke of his fear
I felt also
As he spoke of his disappointment
I felt concerned.
The silence occurred between us two
We looked at one another and we knew
These words would go no further out into the world
For the trust was of paramount to us two
I wished him the best and sent him my thoughts
I told him I would be thinking of him.
We now both wait
Sharing the load, his worry is halved
I hope.

Today Let It Flow

Just for today
Let it flow
Don't create obstacles on your way
Smile, be pleasant and walk by.
Today is your day
To let things flow
Today I don't want any hassle or untoward feelings
For today I want to be left alone
A day of reflection and to flow.
Some days challenges will come your way
But until that happens
Let it flow.

Tomorrow

Tomorrow who do you want to be?
You can be whoever you want to be
A new day, fresh start
For yesterday is in the past
It no longer exists
If you hurt another in the time that no longer exists
Some energy might still remain
You can rectify this energy by infiltrating positive light
Counteracting the stagnate energy with a good deed
It's hardly rocket science.
Life is all about balancing energies
Not being consumed with negative scenarios
But also being aware a balance has to exist
Or how are we to learn?
Thought provoking!
So who are you going to be tomorrow?
The fun loving light energy or the grey cloud that
dampens all around?

Trees

Look at the beautiful trees
Gently swaying in the breeze
Swaying in perfect unison
Gently brushing against another's leaves
So gently, almost as one
For Mother Nature designed the trees to work together.
To shelter others from the rain
Cool the vulnerable in summer
And protect the innocent from the harsh wind.
So valuable our trees
They even filter our air for us
Therapeutic on the eye, uplifting for the soul
A feeling of serenity and being one
When spending time amongst the many.
We are so fortunate to experience and see the beauty of
our land
So, so fortunate
Not to be taken for granted.
A time to make that stand
A stand for the silent trees swaying in the breeze.

True

Always remain true
Especially true to yourself
Whatever your values and beliefs
Always remain true.
True to yourself, true to others, true to all.
Truth and honesty will always surface
This is the law of the universe, it is a must.
Without truth what would our world consist of?
Very little, extremely bleak
A world where few would want to exist
Apart from those who don't care.
The truth can also hurt
But in the long run creates healing,
Evaluation and observation of one's life.
Always choose your words kindly
For truth isn't the gateway and right to hurt another
But gently guide and nurture.
Truth as important as love
For life is pointless without both in one's life.

Trust

Trust the hardest gift to learn
Even harder when once one trusted
Only to be betrayed
I will never trust again
We hear time and time again
But one does with time, nurture and most important
pure
love.
Trust a funny word
Allowing one's guard down
Bearing all including the soul
How beautiful to allow others to see your inner beauty
A pure energy shining through
For so many have never experienced the freedom of
this
joy
How lucky are you?
To be honoured to be set free from all the diversity
Trust my dear
For you will again
For to trust in life of different kinds
Will come your way
Just not when one is expecting it
Trust!

Unity Of Man

A world where colour, creed and religion doesn't exist
A world where everything is balanced and lives in
harmony
A haven where Mother Nature roams freely without
the
destruction of life
A peace and tranquillity words cannot describe for
there
are no words for such a humble existence
No anxiety, no fear of the unknown
For the unknown is now known
A completion and total acceptance of one's self
The true light that flickers within
Has now been set free
For all to see
But more important
You to see
The beautiful pure love of light
You had hidden from the world.

Unity

Unity helping one another upon your paths
Doesn't mean you have to always agree
For life would be rather dull if we all conformed
The world would consist of very little learning
For through different opinions comes understanding and
acceptance
Igniting thought provoking views, otherwise you might never have thought of
A unity of bonding, accepting and respecting
We are all unique and special
Whether that be the grumpy opinionated person
Who we learn to embrace for we know deep down
There is a light of love buried within their heart
They just got a little hurt upon their way.

Vulnerable

Once upon a time
There was a strong athletic, handsome man
Everyone admired from a distance
He was the talk of the town
Women would swoop over him.
He was quite arrogant, as he knew it.
As time went on, so did life
Then came old age.
People began to no longer notice
No one would stop and stare
Almost as though he wasn't there
He became vulnerable.
Remember these words
Vulnerability will occur to us all throughout life
Never judge a book by its cover
And every book you judge has a story.

Warmth

One of the simplest possessions one can obtain
But so often taken for granted.
That is until the luxury is removed
One suddenly feels cold and vulnerable
Not nice to feel the chill deep within your bones
See the breath out in the open.
Struggling to find enough items to fend off the chill
Running out of layers to protect you from the harsh
reality
of the moment.
Too cold to move, too cold to remain still
Feeling damn right miserable.
Someone offers you shelter from the cold
You are offered warmth
Not just warmth of heat but also the warmth of a
smile.
Pure bliss, just for the present moment
King or queen of yourself
Empowered and honoured by another.
The power of warmth so many take for granted.

Weep

Weep you must for tears are precious
A precious commodity one very rarely
Allows oneself to expose.
Let the tears flow free
For another will never condemn
The freedom of emotions.
Another will also feel your despair
Silently watch and care.
Freedom to weep is a gift
It is how we were made to share
Share our vulnerability with others who also care.
Never restrain the tears within
For manifestation deep within will result
In anger, anxiety and ill health.
Nobody said one mustn't cry
So cry with all your soul
Let the emotions free to roam
Then you are free to roam this land
With conviction and an energy to share.

What Is It That Worries You?

An unsettled feeling inside
An impatience and desire
A longing to strive forward
But a deep concern within not to dare
For once the leap of faith occurs
There is no turning back
For the world will finally know you
The beautiful innocent courageous you
With such gifts stoved upon
Intrigued by many, ridiculed by few
For even the non believer will choose to by pass
For it will only be the hurt and wounded souls who will attach with venom
But these dear are few
They are to be sent love for on their paths they have experienced little
Find a place in your heart to understand the hurt of these
For they mean no harm to you, as they speak words of only self destruction
Never fuel their fires but listen tentatively and see the wounded child within
If this silence empowers them then let it be

For these wounded souls search for love
Remember these words and unbeknown to them your
work will have been done.

Who Knew?

Who knew you were so talented
Who knew?
For you kept your talent and aspirations so quiet
This world and time is a place of wonder
Wonder that is to be shared.
A sharing to all
Those who are truly gifted have an obligation to share
Maybe help another
One who is gifted in the same way
Another who also doesn't feel comfortable talking about
oneself
A fear of being ridiculed
A terror of being labelled
Maybe another will, maybe just maybe they won't.
How are you to know if you don't become exposed?
Expose yourself to the elements of life
Nature can be harsh
But also kind
Rather feel the wind upon one's face
Than the bars upon a cage.

Will You Still Love Me Tomorrow?

I once saw the love in your eyes
Now I watch the passing of time
My memories hold dear within my mind
But I can't remember all the passings of time.
I remember clearly as thou it was today
The twinkle and flicker within your eyes
Oh where did it go, the passing of time?
I remember our embrace and the familiar smell
But it no longer feels like a summer's day.
For no summer day will ever truly exist
Until I am once again with you
I know our paths will meet again
For this thought is of paramount.
This thought is more than I can describe
Because I know deep down
You are by my side
I dream you are lying by my side
It's so real it makes me cry
Cry with sadness but also joy
For I know I am one, but will become one of two.

Wings

You can all fly at any time
Either with imagination or desire
You all have wings to fly from one situation to the next.
Fly high, for there are no limits
You find yourself in an unbearable situation
Just for a moment allow yourself the freedom to fly, fly
away.
Where to?
You choose for you have wings to expand
Expand them with the mind.
Yes you have to come back to reality
But fly you must for when one returns
Things are clearer.
The freedom to breathe, absorb and take yourself away
from the moment.
You all have wings
All capable of flying away but you must remember
As one flies throughout this world
The turbulence of the wind, rain and storms are always present
It's just allowing yourself
To coast from one experience to another.

Work

You can achieve if you work hard
With hard work and determination rewards will come
your way
If you don't quite achieve the final destiny
You will be rewarded on your way
Hard work will always open doors
Doors of opportunity or perhaps self discovery
But hard work never goes unnoticed
At times you might think so
Trust good can only come from dedication
What is it that one is prepared to work so hard for?
If it's a dream or destiny
Work from the heart and honourably
If you strive for success that will benefit others too
Your odds of succeeding will come through
One thing you might be worth asking yourself
Is this hard work for something heartfelt?
For if just for money, can be obtained
But the satisfaction won't fulfil all your days
Ask yourself truthfully what you are working so hard
for
If it excites you and lightens the soul
Then continue to work night and day.

Worry

Worry here, worry there, and worry everywhere
So much energy
Worrying about our young
A natural occurrence for loving parents
But worry no more
For the energy is wasted
For each soul within a child will shine through.
Your child was born, with a beautiful soul
One of wisdom and purity all rolled into one
Your job as a parent is to nurture and love
Guide on the path
But the ability to step back and let them be who they
are
So much teaching on conforming to society's demands
How about teaching that child
To embrace who they are?

You Have My Heart

I give you my heart
I would give you my soul
If only to make the world a better place for you.
I love you more than the air one breathes
The starry stars bright at night
I love you more than the universe and beyond.
I give you hope when all around appears bleak
I listen when you are weak
When anger takes control, I remain present
But when you weep, I weep also
Silent tears that streak
Please remember the marks may remain deep
But the marks upon one's face will dissolve
Like everything in life
There has to be the cycle of life
One of love as one of despair
The cycle will always continue to care.

You're Not Listening

You're not listening
Why is that so?
For you know what is right and wrong
So why are you not listening?
If you are waiting for another to make everything alright
You'll be waiting a long time
Perhaps days and nights
You have the keys to open the doors
For the path is going nowhere, that's for sure.
Once you open the door
You'll be on your way
Back on route on your summer's day.
Time to listen to yourself
When will it be, when you're on your way?
For remember another cannot open the door
For you have the keys
To your final destiny.

Printed in Great Britain
by Amazon

56505443R00129